Let's Talk About
BEING MESSY

Let's Talk About
BEING MESSY

By JOY BERRY

Illustrated by John Costanza
Edited by Kate Dickey
Designed by Abigail Johnston

GROLIER ENTERPRISES CORP.

Let's talk about BEING MESSY.

You are being messy when you

- spill food on your clothes, or
- drop food on the furniture or floor.

You are being messy when you

- walk into clean areas with dirty feet,
- touch furniture or walls with dirty hands, or
- sit on furniture while wearing dirty clothes.

You are being messy when you

- do not put your trash in trash cans, or

- do not put your garbage
  in garbage disposals or containers.

You are being messy when you

- do not put things away after you use them,

- do not put things where they belong, or

- do not put things away neatly.

You can make a mess with things such as crayons, paints, ink pens, clay, or glue. You are being messy when you get these things on your clothes or your surroundings.

A mess can be *displeasing*.

Most people enjoy cleanliness, order,
and beauty. A mess is not clean.
It is not orderly. It is not beautiful.
A mess does not make people happy.
It usually makes them unhappy.

A mess can be *frustrating*. It is upsetting when you cannot find something you want or need. It is hard to find something when

- there is so much clutter you cannot see where things are, or

- something is not where it is supposed to be.

A mess can be *destructive*.

- Your clothes and surroundings
  can be ruined by messy stains.

- Things that are left out
  can be damaged accidentally.

- Things that are not put away carefully
  can be ruined.

A mess can be *dangerous*.

- People can slip and possibly fall because of messy spills.

- People can trip over things that are out of place.

Messes can be

- displeasing
- frustrating
- destructive
- dangerous

This is why you should not be messy.

Many accidents become messes. You can avoid accidental messes by *being careful*.
There are other things you can do to avoid messes.

To avoid a mess:

- Cover yourself before you eat
  or do a project that might be messy.
  Put something like a napkin, apron,
  or smock over your clothes.

- Cover the area in which you plan to work.
  Put something like newspapers,
  an old sheet, or a tablecloth on the furniture
  or floor.

To avoid a mess:

- Keep yourself and your clothes
  as clean as possible.

- Wash your dirty hands before you touch
  clean things.

- Get the dirt, mud, or sand off your feet
  before you walk into a clean area.

To avoid a mess:

- **Do not litter**. Put your trash in a trash can and your garbage in a garbage disposal or container.

- **Put things away**. Put things where they belong after you use them. Put things away neatly.

You and the people around you will be happier
if you avoid being messy.